Winnie the Pooh

It's Fun to Make a New Friend

ADVANCE PUBLISHERS

Advance Publishers, L.C.
1060 Maitland Center Commons, Suite 365
Maitland, FL 32751 USA

10 9 8 7 6 5 4 3 2 1
ISBN-10: 1-57973-395-6

One winter morning, Pooh threw open his window. "Piglet!" he cried. "It's finally here!"

"What is?" asked Piglet. He stood on tiptoe and tried to look out.

WINTER

In many places, winter is the coldest time of the year. It can get very windy, snowy, and icy outside. Ponds and lakes may freeze and turn to ice.

"The first snowfall of winter!" Pooh exclaimed.

Piglet jumped and jumped, but he couldn't get much higher than the windowsill.

"Maybe the view would be better from outside," suggested Pooh.

TIGERS

Some tigers live in the jungles of Asia. Their stripes and colors help them hide in the tall grass. They stay very quiet when they hunt. They walk very slowly. Then suddenly ... they pounce!

Tigger was already out and about. From the moment he had opened his eyes that morning, he had been bouncing on the snow as if it were a giant trampoline.

When lots of snowflakes fall, they pile up to make a blanket of snow.

SNOW

In cold temperatures, clouds will form ice crystals instead of raindrops. These crystals become heavy and fall to the ground as snow.

Now his enthusiastic bounces were making piles of snow fall off Pooh's roof—and onto everyone's heads!

"Oh, d-d-dear!" cried Piglet. "The snowflakes are awfully heavy this year."

"I don't mind!" cried Tigger. "I love everything about winter! It's the slipperiest, slide-iest season there is! And speaking of slide-iest—there's Christopher Robin's sled!"

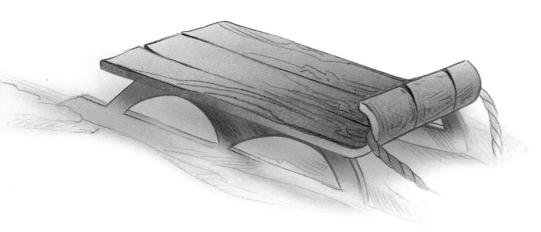

DAYLIGHT HOURS

Winter days are very short. The sun sets early in the evening, and, without the sun's light to warm the air, the temperature gets colder.

If you want to see the lacy design of a snowflake, you have to look fast—before they melt!

SNOWFLAKES

All snowflakes have six sides, but no two snowflakes look exactly alike. When it's very cold out, snowflakes are small, long, and thin. When it's warmer, they're larger and have more detailed designs.

The friends climbed aboard. "Wheeeee!" they cried as the sled glided through the woods. Every now and then, some snowflakes fluttered down. Roo caught them on his tongue.

Pooh and his friends are easy to see, but some animals become almost invisible in winter.

ANIMAL CAMOUFLAGE

Some animals change their appearance in winter. This weasel's brown coat turns white in winter. The white fur helps it blend in with snow and stay hidden from predators. In spring, this weasel sheds its white coat for a brown one again.

After their ride, Piglet and Roo made a pile of snowballs.

"Let's use them to build a snowman!" Roo exclaimed.

But no one could remember how to turn snowballs into a snowman. They asked Owl, but he couldn't recall either.

"I know who can help us," he said.

"Stay right here," he added, flying off.
"I won't be long!"

Owl has a relative who lives in the tundra, one of the coldest places in the world.

SNOWY OWLS

The snowy owl has beautiful white feathers that cover its whole body. Even its beak, legs, and feet have feathers on them! The owl's feathers keep it warm through the freezing tundra winters.

It takes a lot of snowflakes to make a snowball— and even more to make a snowman!

ICE CRYSTALS

Snowflakes begin as ice crystals that are as small as specks of dust. As they fall, the crystals connect to other crystals and form snowflakes. Snowflakes can look like flowers, stars, spiderwebs, or even lightning bolts.

Owl returned with Christopher Robin. The boy rolled snowballs in more snow until they were gigantic! Everyone helped stack them up. Then the friends added a face, arms, a hat, and a scarf.

"How do you do, Mr. Snowman?" said Pooh. "And welcome to the Hundred-Acre Wood. We hope you will be happy here."

"I think he is," said Tigger. "Look at him grin!"

If this snowman wants to go for a walk, he'll need something special on his feet.

SNOWSHOES

There are special shoes for walking in the snow. They're called snowshoes! Snowshoes are big and wide so they don't sink and keep you from sinking into the snow when you walk.

Pooh and his friends get cold outdoors in winter, but this moose stays warm!

MOOSE

Some animals have no trouble living in cold, snowy weather. This moose has a thick, furry coat to keep it warm. It also has wide hooves to help it walk through the snow.

By now the friends were getting cold. They decided they should all go back to Pooh's house for hot cocoa. "Won't you join us?" Piglet asked the snowman.

*Pooh might be standing
on someone's dinner!*

SQUIRRELS

Back in the fall, this
squirrel collected
acorns and buried
them. Now that it's
winter, the squirrel
has plenty to eat. It
can smell the nuts
underground, even
if they're covered
with snow. This
makes it easy for
the squirrel to find
its buried snacks!

"Of course he will!" declared Tigger. "Come on,
buddy boy! You're going for a ride!"
Together, they lifted their new friend and bundled
him onto the sled.

A house made of ice sounds kind of nice!

IGLOOS

In the Arctic, there are some people who live in houses made of snow. These houses are called igloos. Even though they're made using big blocks of snow, igloos keep people warm inside by keeping hot air trapped inside and the cold out.

Soon they arrived at Pooh's house. "Now let's get you inside so you can warm up," declared Pooh. "It's freezing out here!"

Bears make themselves comfortable all winter long.

BEARS

During the fall, bears eat lots and lots of food. Then they're ready to go to sleep for the winter. They curl up inside a cave and sleep for about six months. When spring comes, bears wake up. And they are hungry again!

They carried the snowman in, and settled him by the fire.

"Are you quite comfortable?" Pooh asked his guest.

"I think he might be too comfortable," cried Piglet. "He's sliding right off the chair!"

Melting snow is good for trees, but bad for snowmen!

TREES

In winter, trees are covered with a blanket of snow. They will rest through the winter, until spring comes and the snow melts. Then the trees will start to grow buds and little green leaves once again!

Pooh ran to Christopher Robin for help. "Silly old bear," the boy told him. "Snowmen are made of snow. And snow has to stay cold— or else it melts!"

"Oh, no!" said Pooh.

"Don't worry," Christopher Robin replied.

"We can fix Mr. Snowman up good as new."

Snow turns to water when it melts. Water turns to ice when it freezes.

ICE

Ice is water that has frozen. In very cold temperatures, the water in ponds, lakes, and puddles turns to ice. Ice is smooth and slippery to the touch, and it is usually clear or bluish white.

LADYBUGS

Ladybugs find cozy places in which to spend the winter. They like to snuggle up together in tree bark or under logs. You might find a ladybug in your house looking for a warm place to sleep.

Back outside they all went. They added more snow to their new friend here, there, and everywhere until he looked just fine.

"Won't he be lonely out here all by himself?" asked Piglet.

"What if tomorrow we make a whole bunch of snowmen to keep him company?" asked Christopher Robin.

Everyone agreed that it was a splendid idea.

LIGHT AND DARK SEASONS

The North Pole and the South Pole have times called light and dark seasons. That's because it stays dark outside, even during the day in winter, and it stays light outside even during the night in spring.

The friends bid Mr. Snowman good-bye and began to trudge back home.

After a while, Piglet looked behind him. All he saw was the snowy woods.

"Pooh?" he said.

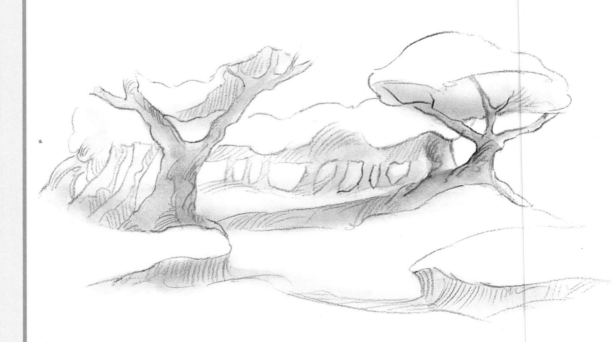

"Down here!" Pooh replied. He had fallen backward into the snow.

"Oh!" cried Piglet with delight. "You're making a snow angel!"

"I am?" Pooh said, flapping his arms and legs about. "I thought I was trying to get up!"

Snow angels aren't the only surprises you can find in the snow!

SNOWDROPS

That flower is called a snowdrop. Snowdrops are one of the first flowers to bloom in the spring. Sometimes they come out so early that there is still snow on the ground!

Just like snowmen, polar bears are right at home in the cold.

POLAR BEARS

Along with their thick fur, polar bears have a 3 inch layer of blubber under their skin. The blubber helps keep them warm while swimming in cold water and walking on ice.

A little while later, the friends were inside, snug and warm. They drank hot cocoa and talked about their adventure-filled day.

"My favorite part was meeting Mr. Snowman," declared Piglet. "There's nothing better than making a new friend."

"Except making him twice!" Tigger exclaimed.